YOUR KNOWLEDGE H

- We will publish your bachelor's and master's thesis, essays and papers

- Your own eBook and book - sold worldwide in all relevant shops

- Earn money with each sale

Upload your text at www.GRIN.com
and publish for free

Bibliographic information published by the German National Library:

The German National Library lists this publication in the National Bibliography; detailed bibliographic data are available on the Internet at http://dnb.dnb.de .

Imprint:

Copyright © 2018 GRIN Verlag
Print and binding: Books on Demand GmbH, Norderstedt Germany
ISBN: 9783668746084

This book at GRIN:

https://www.grin.com/document/432082

Syed Hassan Shah

Quality Assurance in Agile Methodology

GRIN Verlag

GRIN - Your knowledge has value

Since its foundation in 1998, GRIN has specialized in publishing academic texts by students, college teachers and other academics as e-book and printed book. The website www.grin.com is an ideal platform for presenting term papers, final papers, scientific essays, dissertations and specialist books.

Acknowledgment

In the Name of Allah, the Most Beneficent, the Most Merciful.

On the very outset of this report, I would like to extend my sincere & heartfelt obligation towards all the personages who have helped me in this endeavour. Without their active guidance, help, cooperation & encouragement, I would not have made headway in the study.

I am ineffably indebted to my supervisor Dr. Syed Abbas for conscientious guidance and encouragement to accomplish this independent study. I am extremely thankful and pay my gratitude to my faculty guide of SZABIST university Dubai campus for their valuable guidance and support for completion of this study.

I extend my gratitude to department of computer science for giving me this opportunity.

I also acknowledge with a deep sense of reverence, my gratitude towards my parents and member of my family, who has always supported me morally as well as economically.

At last but not least gratitude goes to all of my friends who directly or indirectly helped me to complete this independent study report.

Thanking You

Syed Hassan Shah

Abstract

Quality Assurance activities, in software development, are the backbone of any software development. Quality Assurance activities are not only responsible of product quality, but also for process development quality. In conventional software development Quality Assurance is looked after by a separate team. As the trends of software development moved towards Agile development, Quality Assurance activities also got changed. In Agile development developers perform most of the activities such as close collaboration among developer team; onsite customer and Test Developers. Test Driven Development is the approaches in agile development to achieve better product quality. In this study I highlighted the importance of Quality Assurance in different Agile methodologies. Mindset of Agile development always revolves around product quality but there is much work to be done to impart quality of process in agile development to get it standardized and more organized product. Quality Assurance activities remain centric and focused to testing. In this study I have compared different Agile methodologies and also highlighted the factors of Quality Assurance in each Agile method which can be improve overall software development of any product using Agile method. I proposed to add an extra layer of Quality Assurance in Agile projects. Purpose of inserting an extra layer, is to use the knowledge of Quality Assurance experts to achieve quality product in development process which will results in higher level of product quality.

Keywords: Quality Assurance (QA), Agile Development, Software Process Improvement(SPI)

Table of Contents

List of Figures

List of Tables

List of Abbreviations

QA	Quality Assurance
SQA	Software Quality Assurance
SPI	Software Process Improvement
SDLC	Software Development Life Cycle
IEEE	Institute of Electrical and Electronics Engineers
KIS	Keep It Simple
OOP	Object Oriented Programming
JAD	Joint Application Development
RUP	Rational unified Process
XP	Extreme Programming
YAGNI	You Are not Gonna Need It
FDD	Feature Driven Development
DSDM	Dynamic System Development Method
RAD	Rapid Application Development

Chapter1

Introduction

1.1 Study Overview

When we think about the quality of software, our concern is around the assessment of the software based on certain qualities. The frame work for software development can be adaptable only if it leads to the quality product with high assurance and the concept of how secure quality framework it is [1]. The response of the Quality Assurance is sometimes called as quality framework or it is gradually known as a quality administration framework. It includes administration structure, liabilities, exercises, capabilities and effects of software that guarantee the software production by venture which fulfils the desired quality attributes requirements on which both the client and development organization get agree on it. This implies that a quality framework joins exercises such as examining, analysis, improvement, invalidation of effects, giving inputs, development benchmarks strategies and rules to be followed [2]. The characterized outside quality is based on how software performs in real time situation at operational mode and how valuable it is for its clients, while he inner quality on the other hand centers on the fundamental perspectives that are subordinate on the quality of the code composed. The client centers more on how the computer software works at the outside level, but the quality at outside level can be kept up as it were in case the coder has composed a significant great quality code as appeared in stream chart of inner quality and outside quality components [1]. It is not only reasonable for software developers but also for development teams leaders, project directors, item analysts, improvement supervisors, QA supervisors, QA engineers, specialized scholars and anyone that are a part of software development. This paper will center on how team work can be improve to make all well to arrange, construct, and provide computer software with high Quality Assurance (QA). I will discuss the quality factors of each agile methods that are depend in terms of quality in each agile, will also suggest some practices that can improve the overall life cycle of software development in agile to produce high quality assured product. Hopefully this study will make trends capable in terms of the feasibility of team association in software advancement using agile methodology and will reach to the objective of client fulfilment [3].

1

1.2 Statement of the problem

I will like to quote that "The Agile methodology significantly modifies the Quality Assurance picture by affecting liability of the software for the Client and development team. Needs more work to be done in terms of Quality Assurance in Agile Methodologies [14]. In study I am trying to enquire my work about the following questions:-

i. What is the impact of Agile in the software development life cycle?
ii. Identify the key independent and dependent quality factors of each Agile method that can leads software failure or success during the SDLC in terms of Quality, time and price?
iii. How the current organizations work with agile methods for software development?
iv. What are the basic challenges faces by organization during projects while adopting agile methods?

1.3 Objectives of the study

In spite of the fact that, there are several claims that Agile development is giving us higher quality software. But comparing the studious material with responses of practitioners on software development using agile methods in term of software Quality Assurance, the agile methods are depending on the software value and organizational structure. Some interviews with peers and practically involved people in different organizations experiencing agile methods for software development will assessed to get it, how organizations are practicing SQA in agile methods to improve the product quality in terms of delivery, quality and client requirements. Some of the suggestions will be put forward to organizations that could improve the agile methods and give maximum assurance of quality of any software product during the development stage. Hope my suggestion work will offer assistance to Agile exercises for the development team in current field. In case of how the under process work is done without any break in any step and such agile methods can be profitable in respect to quality and product output.

1.4 Scope and Limitation

The scope limitation must be set in terms of achieving the high quality product that assure the software requirements. Some of the scope limitations may be:

✓ *Zero or small error after Installation:* The main objective of Quality Assurance of any software is to find the errors that can prevent the output. To handle the ability of the software is different in terms of errors, as it leads to the crash of product. So software's failure mostly comes from the avoidance of small bugs in continuously working application.

✓ *Client fulfillment:* In term of SQA the software development must insure the clients' requirements and must exceed their expectations in term of high quality performance and consistent working of product without any defects. Even if system can minimized the errors, still client's satisfaction and requirement fulfillment must be priority.

✓ *Planned well:* Quality Assurance of a software product will ensure that every application must be organized and built in specific manner that meets the requirement of process and desired output. The inter portability of application modules should be well structured to continue the process of development and each application should be transfer to other developer easily.

✓ *Testing:* The objective of testing should be finding the defective bugs created during development stage by programmer. Confidence should be given in terms of quality for development team. Must ensure the end results according to the requirements of client and in terms of product business. Must also insure the requirement specification for a business.

1.5 Significance of the study

Software Quality Assurance (SQA) is defined as a planned and systematic approach to the evaluation of the quality and faithfulness to software product standards, processes, and procedures. This systematic approach is actually quite different in Agile and non-Agile environments. Giving importance to Quality Assurance levels in an Agile methods will improve overall software development process which will leads in end to better software product in terms of meeting clients requirements in term of time, delivery and quality.

Chapter 2

Review of related Literature

My study is based on qualitative approach; keeping all this I concluded in writing all the aspects of Quality Assurance in Agile methodologies. Some interviews were carried out to find the agile methods following in current industry for software development to get maximum Quality assurance of any software product. Peers and practically involved personals such as developers and project managers were interviewed to find the challenges they face during the development process of software in any agile method. In same way literature review was also carried out to collect data of different researchers working in same area of my interest for getting more knowledge about the aspects of Quality Assurance in agile methods. To collect literature of my interest, I use different database sources and resources that can provide data available free on internet. The resources mostly used are as follow:

- ✓ IEEE research papers
- ✓ Google Search engine
- ✓ Google scholar search engine
- ✓ Articles of journals from websites.
- ✓ E-books

Some of the information is provided by peers and practically involved people in current industry. I downloaded free data material and collected data from sources of other personals that is particularly reflect the Quality Assurance and related activities involved in software development life cycle (SDLC) under agile projects. Finding literature related to my study I searched using different keywords by above mentioned search engines and databases available. Most of the areas of research papers and journals such as Abstract, Introduction, future work and conclusion were read for finding the different aspects of Quality Assurance in software development in agile projects. Required information was extracted from the data sources and presented in form of independent study report.

2.1 Quality Assurance

Quality Assurance activities in any software development are the strength of any software development. Quality Assurance activities are not only responsible of product quality, but

4

also for process development of any product to achieve the goals set for customer satisfaction. Presently there are two important methods that are used to find out the quality of the software:

- ✓ Defect Management Approach
- ✓ Quality Attributes approach

2.1.1 Defect Management Approach

Sometimes it is specified that anything that is not with in line with the preconditions of the customer can be considered as an imperfection. Numerous times the development team failed to comes up completely to the necessity of the client, which certainly leads to plan mistake. Other than that, the mistake can be caused due to poor useful logics, off-base coding or dishonourable information dealing among the development team and stakeholders. In arrange to keep a track of irregularity; an imperfection management approach can be connected. In imperfection management; categories of submissions are categorized on seriousness. The number of outputs are checked and activities are taken as per they are categorized by their nature of seriousness. Some of the activities are described in given below figure (2.1)

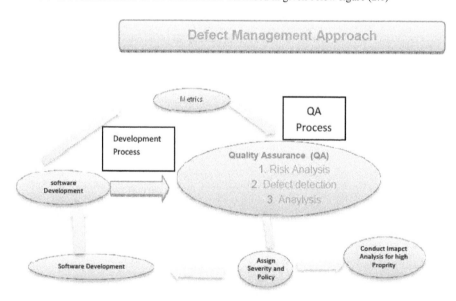

Figure 2.1 Defect Management Approach

5

2.1.2 Quality attribute Approach

Quality attributes are the main themes of the product for which customer are looking for to insure the product values in market as working. This Approach focuses on basic six features which are stated in figure (2.2) given under and each quality attribute is described below

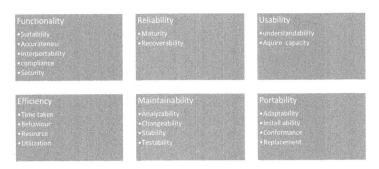

Figure 2.2 Software Quality Attributes

1. Functionality: It refers to comprehensive set of significant functions that are delivered by the software

   ✓ *Suitability:*   functions of the software are suitable or not?

   ✓ *Accurateness:*   implementation of functions are correctly implemented or not?

   ✓ *Interoperability:*   interaction of software with other components.

   ✓ *Compliance:*   are software compliance with essential laws and procedures?

   ✓ *Security:*   how data transactions are secure?

2. Reliability: It refers to the capability of computer software under describing time scale beneath specific conditions. It moreover indicates to the capacity of framework negative response.

   ✓ *Maturity:*   failure recurrence of program

   ✓ *Recoverability:*   response to the failure and how to recover or interpret

3. Usability: refers to the ease of utilize of a function.

   ✓ *Understandability:*   how effortlessly the capacities can be understood

   ✓ *Acquire capacity:*   how much effort the clients of individual level require to put in to get it the functions.

4. Efficiency : It refers to the functionality of different factors and their responses such as

   ✓ Time   : how fast it process and response

6

✓ Behavior   : the way of processing and execution

✓ Resource   : use of resource in efficient way

✓ Utilization: how better the system use the overall allotted resources for a function.

5. Maintainability: refers to the change acceptance and recover the previous active state.

    ✓ *Analyzability: how efficiently analyze the system changes and accept the tolerance.*

    ✓ *Changeability: how much system is able to accept change?*

    ✓ *Stability: do system will stable after change?*

    ✓ *Testability: refers to sureness of the change that it work or not.*

6. Portability: refers to the addition of new hardware and software change.

    ✓ *Adaptability*: how effective the change due to the addition of new hardware and software is effective or acceptable.

    ✓ *Install ability*: how much the hardware/software is synchronized with current.

    ✓ *Conformance*: Does the changes meet the standards followed by a current system?

    ✓ *Replacement:* how much the system reacts to change?

2.2 Importance of Quality Assurance

The Computer Software Quality Assurance (SQA) had get certainly high importance in any software development life cycle due to any agile methodology to insure customer needs and all current rapid changes in software industry that can meet the product in market. QA has worth value in any Software Product Development Life Cycle (SDLC).QA will ensure the fulfilment of the client needs and will provide the product with less number of bugs. Around each movement in software developments either recognized with SDLC or other approaches the QA has importance and make a software product that meets the customer requirements in term of time, delivery and quality [2].

2.2.1   The Quality System of SQA

The system for assuring the quality of a product is more about the reasons that defines the quality components of a product in terms of portability, reusability and conveniences of the product to end user. The framework of quality attributes should be design and well planned that the software development frame work should leads to successful product. SQA examines

7

survey of quality, improvements and highlights the accepting of modern measures, strategies and rules that should be followed during development process [2].

2.2.2 Technical Activities of SQA

In [2] some of the technical activities of SQA system are highlighted which includes Requirement Analysis, Requirement Specification, System design, Detailed design, Acceptance testing and Modular testing

2.2.3 Life Cycle Phase of SQA system Development

Software Development Life Cycle is a subset of the SQA system development life cycle. There are different models for SDLC

2.2.4 Methods of Software Life Cycle development

In the study they choose classic Waterfall model for the Software Development Life Cycle. This indicates the importance of quality assurance in each step of SDLC. Following are the steps discussed during waterfall model of Software Development Life Cycle [2].

- ➢ Requirements Definitions/Analysis
- ➢ Design
- ➢ Code Generation
- ➢ System testing
- ➢ Installation and Conversation
- ➢ Operation and maintenance

In the study they researcher also emphasis that it has a few phases prior to software Development life cycle phases such as

- ➢ Pre-Project Phase

In this phase the organization will initiate its policy and methodology related to quality assurance.

- ➢ Proposal/Contract Phase

During this phase, firstly proposal team develops a proposal draft from the customer requirements documents. Then the contract draft is prepared to customer. After reviewing the contract draft with the customer, a mutually agreed contract that defines sources, timetable and cost estimation for the project is achieved. [2]

8

2.2.5 Standards of SQA

These are the established benchmarks to which software products are associated. It reputable recommended methods for developing software. The role of SQA is to ensure their survival and acceptability. Some of the standards in the study are define as documentation standards, design standards and code standards [2].

2.2.6 Software Quality factors

In [2] it reflects that factors such as correctness, reliability, efficiency, integrity, maintainability, flexibility, testability and usability are the software quality factors which can enhance the product image.

2.2.7 Principle of Quality Development Process

In [2] the researcher highlighted seven principles of quality development process. These principles will lead the maturity of the product in the market and will meet the standards of software development as well as it will meet the requirements of the customer. Each step has an important part in development process to make the software according to specified benchmarks. Following are the steps with its key concepts [2]

- ✓ The **First** Principle: *The reason it all exists*
- ✓ The **Second** Principle: *Keep it Simple(KIS)*
- ✓ The **Third** Principle: *Maintain the vision*
- ✓ The **Fourth** Principle: *What you Produce, Other will Consume*
- ✓ The **Fifth** Principle: *Be Open to the Future.*
- ✓ The **Sixth** Principle: *Plan Ahead for Reuse.*
- ✓ The **Seventh** Principle: *Think*

2.2.8 SQA Methodologies

Software testing is as much an art as a science. In large complex application, such as operating systems, it's practically impossible to iron out every single bug before releasing it both from the difficulty and time constraint point of view. Different software applications require different approaches when it comes to testing but some of the most common task in software QA includes are Peer Review, Validation Testing, Data Comparison, Stress testing, Conformance testing, Load testing, Usability testing and Robustness testing.

Chapter 3

Material and Methods

3.1 SDLC and Agile

Software Development Life Cycle (SDLC) is the complete structure that should be followed to develop the software product while Agile is the method of implementing the development stages in different scenario.

3.1.1 Introduction to SDLC

This is sometimes also called Product Life Cycle. For every software product development a lot of processes and activities are involved, to make is all in stream line to make the outputs interrelated in such a way that the time delay should be minimized and should not make the other processes wait. The development processes of software are come into software process models. These models describe the orders of phases for the entire lifetime of a product. Therefore it is called Software Development Life Cycle (SDLC). It includes software specification, software design, implementation, validation, verification and the most important is its Quality Control. There are various process models for SDLC is in use such as Waterfall model, Spiral Model and Reuse Orientation Model.

3.1.2 Definition of Quality and Agility

Agility is common refers to the readiness to motion while Quality is generally refers to Characteristics of a product. In the study the researchers highlighted definitions of **Quality** and **Agility** by different authors. Some of the definitions by the authors are given in the table below

Table 3.1 Definition of Quality and Agility

Attribute	Authors	Definitions
Quality and Agility	Meyer	Define software quality to an adaptive number of quality factors as defined by McCall.
	McCall	The quality factors defined are Correctness, robustness, extendibility, reusability, compatibility, efficiency, portability, integrity, verifiability and ease of use etc.

	Pressman	He agrees to Crossby and defines quality as "Comprehensive to explicitly stated functional requirements, explicitly documented development standards, implicit characteristics that are expected of all professionally development software's".
	SomerVille	Defines quality as software management process concerned with ensuring that software has a low number of defects and that it reaches the required standards of maintainability, reliability and portability so on.
	Pfleeger	He agrees with Garvin who views quality from five different perspectives: 1) The Transcendental 2) User View 3) Manufacturing 4) Product View 5) The value Based View.
Agile Quality	Amber	Considers agile quality to be a result of practices such as effective collaborative work, incremental development, and iterative development as implemented through different techniques such as refactoring, test driven development, modeling and effective communication.
	McBreen	Agile quality assurance as the development software that can respond to change as the customer requires it to change.

Most of the researchers are agree on the consensus that the quality is conformance to customer needs. Many researchers enhance this view to define quality as characteristics bear by the software product, which reflects the needs specified by the customer

3.2 Agile Methodology

Agility has presently gotten to be imperative with developing elements in commerce all over in arrange to reply quickly to the changes needs of their clients while creating great quality computer program at a quicker rate. Agile computer program advancement speaks to a major conventional, plan-based approach of computer program building to more esteem and client driven [7]. Numerous organizations now a days are confronting the challenges that how do we guarantee in agile the originality of vast predictable Quality Assurance hones that have, in past demonstrated of overwhelming conventional Quality Affirmation hones that have, in past demonstrated to be productive are no longer fitting totally with in agile environment.

3.2.1 Twelve principles behind the Agile Methodology

1. Highest priority is to delivery product in time with fulfillment of clients requirements.
2. Changes should be welcomed even in last stages, that will advantages customers needs
3. Delivery of software should be time lined into week or months with reference to short time schedules.
4. The developers and business people should work together.
5. Support should be given to each motive individual to make the work done in good manner.
6. Sponsors, developers and users should be able to maintain pace.
7. Software working is prior base of measurement.
8. Face to face conversation should be more effective.
9. For enhancing agility, continuous attention should be given to technical assistance.
10. Simplicity of doing work is to get maximum job done.
11. Self-organized team will produce best architectures, requirements and design teams.
12. Regular plans will reflects how the team work is going on and according to that teams can be managed.

3.2.2 QA in Agile

There may be various components that can be assessed in term of quality assurance in any agile methods. Each Agile method must have some dependent and independent factors that can affect the quality of product in terms of in time delivery, cost and usability. Some of the quality factors such as cost, reusability, portability, compatibility, maintainability and robustness etc. which can be taken under consideration to achieve software with high quality in agile method. There are always some functional attributes and non-functional attributes of any software development framework. So some of the above mentioned quality factors are discussed in below table with proposed methods as follow:

Table 3.2   QA in Agile

Quality Factor	Suggested Methods
Compatibility	Platform independence can be achieved by Multiple methodologies especially Open Source Development Methodology. Object oriented (OO) design method can also help and is common practice.
Cost effectiveness	Iterative and Incremental nature will help to achieve cost effectiveness by delivering the prioritized requirements in small increments.
Correctness	Involve active involvement of the customer
Ease of Use	Active Involvement of the customer also increases the understanding of the system thus increasing in ease of use of the system when designing its interface. Interface is highly important when web layouts are designed. Scrum, XP (Extreme Programming), RUP (Rational Unified Process) and JAD(Joint Application Development) Techniques can be useful to achieved it easily.
Extendibility	OOP design, OCT and Modular Development help to cater changes requirements with greater flexibility.
Maintainability	Modular Design and Compatibility between interfaces help to achieve maintainability. Feature Driven development and Crystal Methodology play important role.
Performance	Sprint, OOP design, Code ownerships and Common class activities can help to increase performance.
Portability	Distributed computing and web service design has increased Portability.
Reusability	OOP design is based on the principle of reusability. Organization with agile methodology should keep track of all design increments to make them available in short time boxes.
Robustness	It can be assured by following development standards. While robustness is always be implicit as it cannot be explicit stated.
Timeliness	Interactive development and Short cycles are followed to

	achieve timeliness.
Validation and Verification	Unit testing, integration testing and regression testing and interference testing are commonly followed.

3.3 Traditional Methodology

The traditional methodologies for the development of software have focused on Waterfall approach. While the rapid change in the requirements under influence of market values related to customer requirements, dynamic infrastructure of corporate organization, comprehensive need for short time deliverables and highly variants in speed of advance technologies and tools added the aggressive pressure to sustain in market. As a result many organizations adapted agile method for the development of software. In fact the agile development is popular for quality delivery of the project in small deliverables [11].

3.3.1 Traditional VS Agile

Traditional quality Assurance is based on reporting and they depend on heavy weight inspection methods, while Agile quality assurance methods are based on daily built in activities. In Agile environment quality Assurance activities should be integrated with in day-to-day activities so that flow of process should be in streamline to fulfil the needs for improving the quality of product. Some answers to the questions mentioned below are discussed by a researcher in a paper [8].

> How we can manage the quality of software in Agile?
> Which practices of Agile will ensure the software quality?
> What are the key drivers of Quality in Agile?

In the study the researcher highlights the debates on agile methodologies, stated that quality assurance practices have gained less attention while agile methodologies has been on the development of activities and an overall picture is somehow missing. Some authors reported that QA practices are constructed into XP process like a spiral model adopts them. Study by Noura, et al [8,9] supports that quality in Agile projects is the key contributor to project success. Another study by Ahmed et al [8,10] also reports key attributes such as participation of stakeholders, Self-organized teams and size of teams etc. have impact both on productivity and quality of the finished product.

14

In Agile methodologies the key to successful quality Assurance (QA) are the frequent changes. Therefore the importance of Quality Assurance is important for the quality of software product irrespective of the development process one chooses.

3.4 Agile Development and Quality Assurance

Agile method is used to develop software under particular pattern that can leads the development of product in such a way that meets the requirement of client and produce the product in good manner in time. Quality Assurance will guarantee each step of development process with less errors and delay. QA will also assure compatibility and inter relationships of each individual team for producing same product in specified timeline.

3.4.1 Agility

The word Agility refers to the status of movement or status of something in motion according to some dictionaries [24]. The agility in terms of software development process reflects to the entire continuous process that integrates all the steps together to achieve the software product. Erickson [25] characterized agility as "conventional software development, changes in client necessities, quickened delivery in due dates and the techniques that influence the development of software product".

3.4.2 Types of Agile Methodologies

There is a lot of software development Life cycles that comes under the umbrella of agile methods. Some of the agile methods explained below.

3.4.2.1 Extreme Programming (XP)

Extreme Programming agile method aims to provide high feature software. It is applicable when software have a characteristics that describes such as dynamic changes in software requirements, risk of new technology integration in fixed time period and co located small team etc. It mostly have short development life cycle that focus on needs of today rather than the coming up in the future, which is somehow also called YAGNI approach. It means "You Are not Gonna Need it".

3.4.2.2 Scrum

Scrum agile methodology on three specific roles of product owner, scrum master and scrum team. Product owner should been in up to date about the product in priority based, scrum master handles the sprint which is actually a time scale job to be done to achieve specific goal set by scrum master under scrum team, scrum team is product development team that actually preparing the results and completing task in given time called sprint. Scrum performance is totally depends on the value of sprint, the more accurate sprint timing set to achieved the task the product development become smooth otherwise the delay of the product may happen if sprint is able to achieve its target.

3.4.2.3 Crystal Methodology

In crystal methodology each work is distributed by the nature of its hardness, each crystal is scheduled according to the natural of its working and development. Some of the standard crystals are defined that automatically lies under the hardness of the task under agile method, such as crystal clear, crystal yellow and crystal red etc. The layers are called crystal family.

3.4.2.4Kanban Methodology

The word "Kanban" is used by Japanese in TOYOTA Company for the daily routine working which is carried out in the company. The Kanban actually means the "billboard" where the daily routine works is pasted. In Kanban agile method each tasks are individual assigned to team and progress of the work is showed through the daily, weekly or monthly bases. Each department is doing their work separately no one is dependent to each other.

3.4.2.5Feature Driven Development (FDD) Methodology

The name of the agile it-self reflects the meaning and working of the agile process. FDD Methods execution depends on the features having high priority. The feature is assumed be the high priority in term of complexity, coding, application or client requirement etc.

3.4.2.6 DSDM Methodology

DSDM stands for Dynamic systems Development Method. An agile method initially used for software development early in 1990's. DSDM originally gives discipline to the rapid application development (RAD) method. But later it becomes a famous approach for project management and delivery of solution rather than code creation and software development. It was mostly used for non-IT projects. This method also covers a high range of activities inside the project life cycle and includes well-built foundation and governance, which separates it from some other agile methods. It is incremental and iterative approach that includes high involvement of customer/user.

3.5 Methods

Study is based on qualitative approach. Information is collected through literature review approach. Method of study is to review the related information available in form of research papers, articles and blogs that describe the problem definition. The major material related to topic in the study is as follow Quality Assurance, Importance of Quality Assurance, SDLC and Agile, Traditional Methodology, Agile Development and Quality Assurance.

3.5.1 Qualitative Approach

My research topic and focus area is dealing with theoretical conceptual than statistical data. I was needed to elaborate the important concept s and the aspects of Quality Assurance(QA) in some of the agile development methods to identify the dependent factors of QA in my area of interest.

3.5.2 Informal Interviews

I conducted formal interviews with little software Quality Assurance professional and developers of software in different organization as well as the peers who are involve in the type of industry where agile methods are used for developing software. Group discussions were taken with colleagues regarding gaining maximum quality assurance during agile development of any software. Purpose of these formal interviews was to remain focus on the dependent factors that can be found out in terms of improving quality assurance in different agile methods.

Chapter 4

Results and Findings

In study different scholars papers are reviewed with respect of quality assurance in agile methods and some of the major descriptive points are evaluated to describe the importance of each agile method for development of software with their own strengths, weakness, and effectiveness and focus areas.

4.1 Trends in Agile Methodologies

Table 4.1 Scrum

Scrum	

Description	• Complex set of development principles.
	 • Focus on management aspects of projects.
	 • Operate in brief iterations (sprints) for the advancement of collective work.
	 • Full team work depends upon three main Human power
	    ✓ Product Owner
	    ✓ Scrum Master
	    ✓ Scrum Team

Effectiveness	• This methodology enables management teams to spot problems at the development stage. • Promotes transparency among the colleagues. • Its good practice is the daily standup meetings a time boxed daily event, where all team members discuss work progress and possible obstacles.
Strengths	• Solution definition led by it directed development team. • Priorities based on business value.
Weakness	• Terminology and practices oriented towards technical teams. • Little business control over managing and prioritizing features different to scope.
Focus On	✓ Sprints timing. ✓ Daily meeting about the work progress. ✓ Management aspect of Projects

Table 4.2 Crystal

Crystal	
Description	• A Human-Powered **Methodology** for Small Teams. • Family of small agile methodologies based on work weight such as ✓ Crystal Clear ✓ Crystal yellow ✓ Crystal Red etc. • Crystal family suggests that each project is unique and requires the application of different processes, practices and policies.
Effectiveness	• Early delivery of working software, frequency, less bureaucracy. • High involvement of user. • It is perceived as one of the most lightweight agile methodologies. Some of the key properties are ✓ Frequent delivery ✓ Reflective improvement ✓ Close or osmotic communication ✓ Personal safety ✓ Easy access to expert users ✓ Technical environment with automated tests, configuration management, and frequent integration
Strengths	• Family of methodologies designed to scale by project size and criticality. • Only methodology that specifically accounts for life critical projects. • As project size grows, cross-functional teams are utilized to ensure consistency. • An emphasis on testing is so strong that at least one tester is expected to be on each project team. • The "Human "component been considered for every aspect of the project support structure.
Weakness	• Experts all team members to be co-located may not work well for distributed teams. • Adjustments area required from one project size/structure to an order to follow the prescribed flavors of crystal for that project size/criticality.

	• Moving from one flavor of crystal to another in mind project does not work, as crystal was not designed to be upward or downward compatible.
Focus On	✓ Promotes early and frequently delivery of working software. ✓ High User Involvement. ✓ Removal of distraction. ✓ Small teams. ✓ Interaction ✓ Community ✓ Skills ✓ Talents ✓ Communication

Table 4.3 Extreme Programming

Extreme Programming (XP)	
Description	• It involves a high degree of participation between two parties in the software exchange customer and developers. • It requires a great level of discipline, as well as plenty of involvement from people beyond the world of information technology.
Effectiveness	• Emphasizing the most useful features of a given software product. • High level of collaboration a minimum of up-front documentation. • It's an efficient and persistent delivery model.
Strengths	• Most widely known and adopted approach. • Business ownership of features priority, developer ownership of estimates. • Pair programming increase knowledge increase.
Weakness	• Documentation primarily through verbal communication. • Difficult to accommodate architectural or design concerns.
Focus On	✓ High degree of participation between Customer and Developers. ✓ Emphasizes on the most useful features of the product.

Table 4.4Kanban

Kanban	
Description	• It synchronizes quality of stock with the availability of given product. • Its bases its production frequency on consumption rates. • Working progress is updated on chart. • Each individual working in its own stream.
Effectiveness	• It facilitates production and an effective mean for generating improvements. • It limits the amount of work that can be delay in an unfinished state, which helps prevent production chains from getting backlogged.
Strengths	• Change can be made any time. • Remove activities that do not add value scalable.
Weakness	• No prescribed roles. • No time boxing notion. • Limit work in progress. • Based on what you do today.
Focus On	✓ *Individual work output.* ✓ *Synchronization of work done by each team.*

4.2   New Development Approach in Organizations

The development frame work is the industrial responses for more investigation in this area. The unified agile methodologies help in solution of the problems which can occur to the bulky products. This is an easy approach in terms of cost and resources, so is more manageable. This frame work is also beneficial for both larger organizations as well as for individual product team delivers. It can be expected that the combination of Agile and SDLC, can create slimmer and more meticulous product derivation process [23].

4.3   Spreading Trend

Software development industry comprises the agile methodologies. The value of these methodologies in reforming software processes directed the organizations to consider the use of Agile method to non-software project as well as vast processes based software's, a substantial research exists on software development and agile methodologies which can improve the process of software development [24].

4.4 The Bright Side of Agile Development

Agile development methods which are hired from the software industry are now being used by a few of built-up companies for physical products. Agile methods, which contain different parameters, are normally put in with some or all of the stages of a current stages based systems. Agility shows improvements in terms of time and productivity, and shows faster responses to conditions of the market and customer needs. Nevertheless, they also recognized many tasks in executing hybrid systems. Based on case companies 'involvements, my study will provide suggestions of Agile methods that can provide a hybrid systems with maximum quality assurance [25]. Some of the highlighted useful factors such as flexibility, transferring of knowledge, Project control, increased productivity, early finding of feasibility and bugs and high quality product which can be experienced by agile practitioners [23].

4.5 Challenges Adopting Agile Development

Quicker customer feedback, early release and its interactive methods are some characteristics of agile methodology due to which it's getting popular. After reviewing papers of investigators and interviewing the teams responsible for development of a software product and planning analysis , I concluded that following challenges are in agile use on QA:-

- ✓ Recognize correct agile methodology.
- ✓ Planning and application for the required tools or stages.
- ✓ Defining the teams and process roles.
- ✓ Planning of Testing and Automation (when and how).
- ✓ User feedback and customer idea deadlocks.
- ✓ Lack of communication and changing necessities.
- ✓ Dependency of development stages.

4.6 Improvement of QA in Different Agile

After the study I come to a point that Agile method for any particular work depends on structure of organization and conceded work, under different conditions. There is no exact agile method for any specific frame work. The only I can suggest some of the points that can improve the agile methods in regards to assure quality maximum of any software product. Some of the suggested points are:-

- QA teams must focus the most dependent factor in software development that can influence overall process.
- QA team in agile needs to be able to respond quickly according to changing requirements.
- QA team needs detail of each necessity to start testing.
- A proper communication between designers, project managers and QA teams.
- Continuous contact between developers and product owner.
- Time to time Automation skills can be a great help in any agile project.

Chapter 5

Conclusion and Future Work

5.1 Conclusion

Though this study I concluded that the development of agile concentrates on quality of process to manage the measurements in way that give high quality product. Rather focusing on customer's technical education we should use the teams who are expert in minimizing the gap between the demands related to social and system requirements. By Integrating knowledge of QA in agile projects for the development of complex systems can be maximized in terms of measurements and standardization. No doubt testing plays a key role in QA but quality can be attributed more than testing. The quality of process and product can be increased by taking the capabilities of tester or designer and organizational knowledge. Pair programming and test driven development can be best approaches but in case of agile development they must be calculated and standardized to attain high quality product and sustain the taken measurements well in time.

5.2 Future Work

In my studies, formal interviews and literature review was done. If this research be conducted over large scale more effective results can be achieved. Furthermore if this research involves statistical analysis that involves testing of quality assurance in each stage of agile can bring more clear picture of each dependent factor for achieving maximum quality assurance QA) in any agile method. My future work includes an on-going study into the benefits of combining Agile and SDLC approaches and the validation of the current frameworks in the industry, particularly in terms of cost, quality and time. I understood that higher quality of any product and process can be achieved through adding one more layer of QA. But as it's not a final solution and it needs much research work to be done that can be effective and fruitful for projects based on agile development. Testing is the area where most of the researchers done their work to get high value for quality assurance in an agile methods. So to achieve high quality, organized and standardized development, we must involve quality experts who have extensive knowledge and understanding of quality parameters for that projects that based on agile development.

References

[1]"What is Software Quality Assurance? - International Software Test Institute", *Test-institute.org*,2018.[Online].Available:https://www.testinstitute.org/What_is_Software_Quality_Assurance.php.

[2]C. SenthilMurugan and S. Prakasam, "A Literal Review of Software Quality Assurance", *International Journal of Computer Applications*, vol. 78, no. 8, pp. 25-30, 2013.

[3]M. Habib, "Agile software development methodologies and how to apply them - CodeProject",*Codeproject.com*,2018.[Online].Available:https://www.codeproject.com/articles/604417/agile-software-development-methodology-and-how-t/. [Accessed: 11- Jun- 2018].

[4]"What is Agile? What is Scrum?",*cPrime*, 2018. [Online]. Available: https://www.cprime.com/resources/what-is-agile-what-is-scrum/. [Accessed: 11- Jun- 2018].

[5]P. Sharma and D. Singh, "Comparative Study of Various SDLC Models on Different Parameters", *International Journal of Engineering Research*, vol. 4, no. 4, pp. 188-191, 2015.

[6]"Home ::.IJARCSMS.::", *Ijarcsms.com*, 2018. [Online]. Available: http://ijarcsms.com/. [Accessed: 11- Jun- 2018].

[7]IEEE Computer Society, "Quality Assurance In Agile", Gurgaon, India, 2012.

[8]"The impact of organization, Project and Governance Variables on Software Quality and project Success", 2010.

[9]"A. Ahmed, S. Ahmad, Dr. N. Ehsan, E. Mirza and S. Z. Sarwar, "Agile Software Development Impact on Productivity and Quality," Proceedings of the 2010 IEEE ICMIT, Singapore, 2-5 June 2010, pp. 287-291. - References - Scientific Research Publishing", *Scirp.org*, 2018.[Online]. Available: http://www.scirp.org/reference/ReferencesPapers.aspx?ReferenceID=358697

[10]A. Powell-Morse, "Waterfall Model: What Is It and When Should You Use It?",*Airbrake Blog*, 2018. [Online]. Available: https://airbrake.io/blog/sdlc/waterfall-model.

[11]S. Alam, S. Nazir, S. Asim and D. Amr, "Impact and Challenges of Requirement Engineering in Agile Methodologies: A Systematic Review", *International Journal of Advanced Computer Science and Applications*, vol. 8, no. 4, 2017.

[12]2018. [Online]. Available: https://www.visualstudio.com/learn/what-is-scrum/ (Agile Methodologies).

[13]"What Is Kanban? An Introduction to Kanban Methodology", *VersionOne*, 2018.[Online]. Available: https://www.versionone.com/what-is-kanban/.

[14] Available: https://project-management.com/xp-fdd-dsdm-and-crystal-methods-of-agile-Development/.

[15]"Common Challenges QA Teams Face in Agile Testing and Tips to Overcome Them!",*Medium*, 2018. [Online]. Available: https://medium.com/a3logics-i-pvt-ltd/common-challenges-qa-teams-face-in-agile-testing-and-tips-to-overcome-them-c441e32d2b1b.

[16]"Key Challenges In Agile Implementations On QA Eyes | Xoriant Blog", *Xoriant Blog*, 2018.[Online].Available:https://www.xoriant.com/blog/agile/key-challenges-agile implementations-qa.html.

[17]"The Future of Agile Software Development - Ubie Digital", *Ubie Digital*, 2018. [Online].Available: http://ubie.io/the-future-of-agile-software-development/.

[18]S. Michael Dubakov, "The Future of Agile Software Development | Targetprocess Visual Managementsoftware", *Targetprocess*,2018.[Online].Available:https://www.targetprocess.co/articles/t he-future-of-agile-software-development/.

[19]S. Michael Dubakov, "The Future of Agile Software Development | Targetprocess – Visual management software", *Targetprocess*, 2018. [Online].Available: https://www.targetprocess.com/articles/the-future-of-agile-software-development/.

[20]Ahsan Nawaz, KashifMasood Malik, ", "Software Testing Process in Agile Development"", Blekinge Institute of Technology, Sweden, 2008.

[21]P. O'Leary, F. McCaffery, S. Thiel and I. Richardson, "An agile process model for product derivation in software product line engineering", *Journal of Software: Evolution and Process*, vol. 24, no. 5, pp.561-571, 2010.

[22]L. Rosser, P. Marbach, G. Osvalds and D. Lempia, "7.4.2 Systems Engineering for Software Intensive Projects Using Agile Methods", *INCOSE International Symposium*, vol. 24, no. 1, pp. 729-744,2014.

[23]J. Kisielnicki and A. Misiak, "effectiveness of agile compared to waterfall implementation methods in it projects: analysis based on business intelligence projects", *Foundations of Management*, vol. 9, no. 1, 2017.

[24]P. Martins and M. Zacarias, "An Agile Business Process Improvement Methodology", *Procedia Computer Science*, vol. 121, pp. 129-136, 2017.

[25]O. Salo and P. Abrahamsson, "An iterative improvement process for agile software development", *Software Process: Improvement and Practice*, vol. 12, no. 1, pp. 81-100, 2007.

[26]J. Kisielnicki and A. Misiak, "Effectiveness Of Agile Compared To Waterfall Implementation methods in it projects: analysis based on business Intelligence projects", *Foundations of Management*, vol. 9, no. 1, 2017.

[27]R. Cooper and A. Sommer, "Agile–Stage-Gate for Manufacturers", *Research-Technology Management*, vol. 61, no. 2, pp. 17-26, 2018.

[28]R. Cooper and A. Sommer, "Agile-Stage-Gate: New idea-to-launch method for manufactured new products is faster, more responsive", *Industrial Marketing Management*, vol. 59, pp. 167-180, 2016.

[29]E. Conforto and D. Amaral, "Agile project management and stage-gate model—A hybrid framework for technology-based companies", *Journal of Engineering and Technology Management*, vol. 40, pp. 1-14, 2016.

YOUR KNOWLEDGE HAS VALUE